The Real Scientist

Heave!

Forces and how they move things

Peter Riley

W
FRANKLIN WATTS
LONDON·SYDNEY

Contents

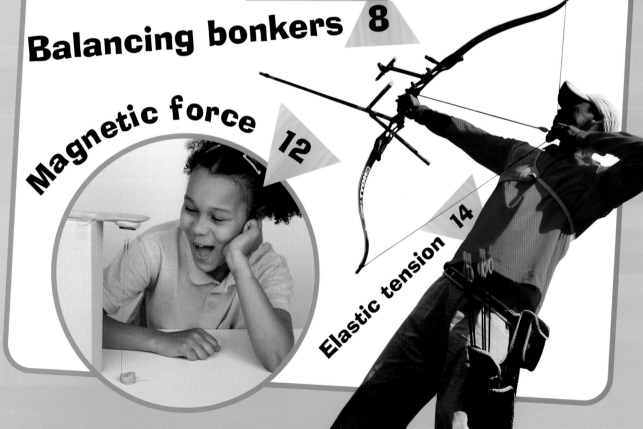

Super forces

Heave – it means to pull as hard as you can when you're trying to move something heavy. Pulling is one of many forces that can cause something to move, change direction, speed up, slow down and stop. A force can even keep something still.

You can see and feel the effects of forces although you will never see the forces themselves. Forces are invisible but real scientists have studied them for centuries and found out lots about them.

This truck-pull event is a strength test. Competitors pull on a rope and drive forwards with their legs to move the truck down the course.

◀ Humans and other animals have muscles, which generate forces to move limbs and bodies.

How to be a real scientist

Real scientists look at our world and try to understand it by thinking about it and performing experiments. You can be a real scientist too! Just look at each topic, read the 'getting going' section and then get experimenting.

Set up a science box
Find a large box, then skip through the pages in this book and look at the things you need to get going and for each activity. Collect them up and put them in your science box.

▶ Observe
Look carefully at whatever you are investigating.

▶ Predict
Guess what will happen before you experiment.

▶ A fair test
If you are comparing how something moves make sure you keep everything the same in your tests except for one thing – such as slope height or the weight of the objects.

▶ Science notebook
You will need a science notebook in which to put information about your investigations.

▶ Record
Write down what happened and perhaps make a drawing in your science notebook.
You could take photographs too or make a video using a camcorder or mobile phone.

▶ Make a conclusion
Compare what happened with your prediction and see if you were right. It does not matter if you were wrong because it helps you rethink your ideas.

▶ Experiments and answers
Follow the steps in the experiments carefully. Use your science skills. There may be extra experiments and a question for you to try. Check all your observations, ideas and answers on pages 28–29.

▶ What went wrong?
Science experiments are famous for going wrong – sometimes. If your experiment does not seem to work, look for this section to help you make it right.

What goes up...

Gravity is the force that makes things fall. When most things fall, they fall straight down – quickly! This makes falling difficult to observe.

About 400 years ago a real scientist called Galileo realised that when something rolls down a ramp it is being pulled by gravity – but it falls more slowly than it would without a ramp. He found that if he let a ball roll down a ramp he could time how fast it moved using a water clock. He compared how balls of different weights fell by letting them roll down a ramp.

Getting going

In this investigation you can find out how the slope of a ramp affects the speed at which things fall. You can also make a set of ramps and set up a table tennis ball so the moving ball can make it swing.

Zig zag ramps

Science box

Large cereal packet, scissors, 2 long cardboard boxes (such as the ones for toothpaste or tomato puree), sticky tape, 2 table tennis balls, thin string or thread.

1

Cut down the side of a cereal packet and lay it flat on the table.

2

Cut up the long cardboard boxes to make four ramps.

3

Arrange the ramps, some long, some short, some steep, some shallow on the cereal packet and hold in place with sticky tape. Stand up the cereal packet.

4

Tape a table tennis ball to the string and then tape the other end of the string so the ball hangs in line with the bottom of the lowest ramp.

▶ **Predict**
Look at the angles of the ramps and predict whether a ball will go fast or slow as it runs down it. What will happen to the other ball when the moving one reaches it?

▶ **Observe**
Release a ball from the top ramp and watch to see if its speed changes on each ramp. What happens to the hanging ball? Check with your predictions. Repeat your experiment twice more and compare the results.

▶ **What's wrong?**
Ball seems to run very fast on all ramps? Try setting them at very different slopes. Ball rolls off the other ramps? Try adding a card edge to the top of the ramps.

▶ **Extra experiment**
Make a set of ramps that lets the ball roll very slowly. Predict what will happen when the ball reaches the hanging ball? Test your prediction.

▶ **Record**
Take photographs of the groups of ramps you make.

▶ **Think about it**
Why are there ramps in a skateboard park?

Balancing bonkers

The force of gravity pulling down on you is called 'weight'. Your weight pulls down from a place inside you called your centre of gravity. Weight pulls down through the base of an object, towards the centre of the Earth.

When the weight pulls down through the base of the object, the object will not fall over even if it is tilted a little. If the object is tilted so that its weight pulls down outside its base, it will fall over when it is released.

▼ This judo throw relies on perfect balance. The man in white keeps his centre of gravity over his left leg so he doesn't fall over.

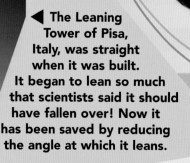

◀ The Leaning Tower of Pisa, Italy, was straight when it was built. It began to lean so much that scientists said it should have fallen over! Now it has been saved by reducing the angle at which it leans.

Getting going

Do full bottles fall over more easily than those that are half full? A scientist needs an angle recorder to find out. If you make one first, see A, you can then test the question.

Testing for balance

A Make an angle recorder

Draw a line near to the bottom of the card and make a dot half way along it. Use the protractor to mark in angle lines 10 degrees apart.

Science box

Card, pencil, ruler, protractor, 500 ml plastic bottle, measuring jug, water, cooking oil, salt, kitchen scales.

1

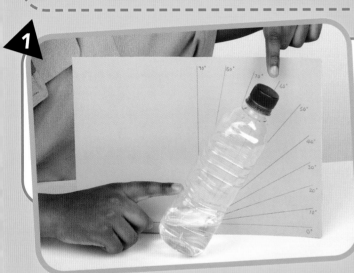

Pour 100 ml of water into an empty bottle then slowly tilt it. Record the angle from the vertical at which it falls over. Add another 100 ml of water and predict what will happen. Keep testing and predicting until the bottle is full.

▶ **Predict**
After you have recorded the angle with the first volume of water, predict the angle you will be able to tip the bottle when a second volume of water is added. Repeat until the bottle is full. Do your predictions get more accurate?

▶ **Record**
Use a mobile phone or camcorder to video a stage of the experiment as you push the bottle over.

▶ **Think about it**
How does increasing the amount of liquid or solid in the bottle alter its centre of gravity? What would happen if you repeated step 1, but with the bottle upside down? Try using a different shaped plastic bottle.

2

Now repeat step 1, but use a different liquid, such as cooking oil.

3

Repeat step 1, but use a solid, such as salt. Add 50 g each time and record your results.

Bridge destruction

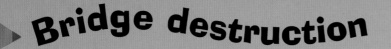

Gravity is a really powerful force – and if things aren't built properly with the right materials they'll come crashing down. Bridges are some of the most amazing, gravity-defying structures built by humans. They have to withstand lots of different forces.

When a bridge is built, it has to support its own weight and the weight of people and vehicles passing across it. There are many types of bridge. Some have arches while others are suspended on cables.

▼ The Golden Gate Bridge in San Francisco, USA, opened in 1937 and spans 1,280 m. The bridge is made from steel and weighs approximately 804,700,000 kg.

Getting going

Bridges have been used for thousands of years to cross ravines and rivers. Does the shape of the bridge affect its strength? And what about the materials it is built from – what effect do they have on the strength?

1

Select the first bridge for testing. Predict how many marbles it will be able to support.

2

Position the bridge on top of the cereal packets.

Science box

A piece of card, corrugated cardboard and a piece of card with sides (try to make the bridges the same size), a yoghurt pot, two cereal packets, marbles (or other small weights).

3

Put the yoghurt pot on top and slowly add marbles. Watch how the bridge bends.

4

Use the same number of marbles to test each bridge. Take a photograph of each one and compare the results.

▶ Predict
Predict the number of marbles each bridge can hold and which will be the strongest bridge and the weakest bridge. Record your predictions then test the bridges.

▶ Record
Take photographs of the bridges when they have sagged. Test your bridges to destruction by noting down how many marbles they can support before they collapse!

▶ Think about it
Look at how corrugated cardboard is made. How do you think this helps cardboard boxes to be strong and yet lightweight?

Magnetic force

The magnetic force was first discovered in a rock called magnetite. The force pulls on iron and steel. The first magnets were made by stroking bars of iron with magnetite.

Real scientists believe that there is a huge ball of iron at the centre of the Earth. The massive amount of iron makes the Earth behave as though it has a huge bar magnet inside it, and the magnetic force from its poles affects the magnets on the Earth's surface. The force of the Earth's magnetism makes free moving magnets, such as a compass, point north and south.

▶ This is the world's biggest magnet – the mega magnet at the European Organization for Nuclear Research – measuring 46 x 25 m.

▶ The Earth has a North Pole and South Pole, just like a magnet, but it is not magnetic!

Getting going

The power of the magnetic force of a magnet can be found by using pieces of card. They are inserted between a magnet and a paperclip and screw until the force can no longer pull on them – see A and B. Don't forget to make a prediction. Then wow your friends with a magnetic force test.

A

Place some thin card between a magnet and a paperclip and screw.

B

Keep adding cards until the paperclip or screw falls away.

Magnet power

Science box

A fridge magnet (or another magnet if you have one), a paperclip, a screw, sheets of thin card, a wooden spoon (or ruler to stick a magnet on), a cereal packet, a length of thread, sticky tape, modelling clay.

1 Attach a magnet to the end of a wooden spoon with modelling clay. Stick the other end of the spoon to the top of a cereal packet.

2 Tie a paperclip to a piece of string and bring it near the magnet. Stick the other end of the string to the table top with more clay. Can you make the paperclip seem to float in the air?

▶ **Predict**
In steps A and B, what will happen if you move the magnet quickly? How many sheets of card will you need before the objects fall away? Will the paperclip or screw fall first?

▶ **Observe**
How many sheets of card does it take to make the paperclip fall away?

▶ **Record**
Write down in your notebook the number of sheets you used. Take a photograph of your floating paperclip.

▶ **Think about it**
What force is the magnetic force pulling against to hold the paperclip in midair?

Magnetic force **13**

Elastic tension

Some materials, such as rubber, are elastic and can be stretched. When you pull on an elastic material a force develops in it called 'tension'. When you let go – twang! Tension pulls the material back to its original shape.

Archers shoot arrows using elastic tension. They pull backwards on the bow string to stretch the bow and create tension. Then they release the string, the arrow is pushed away at speed, and the bow returns to its normal shape.

▲ This bow is made of flexible plastic and has an elastic bow string.

◄ The tension force of this bungee rope is carefully calculated so that the man will not hit the water. He'll just spring back up!

Getting going
An elastic band can be used to fire a missile and a simple device can be made to investigate how the amount of stretch affects how far the missile can travel.

Elastic band rocket

1 Mark the end of an empty clingfilm tube with seven, 1 cm divisions.

Science box

Safety goggles, an empty clingfilm tube, a ruler and pen, an empty kitchen roll tube, an elastic band (with a resting length of about 10 cm).

2 Put on your safety goggles and place the elastic band along the length of the kitchen roll tube.

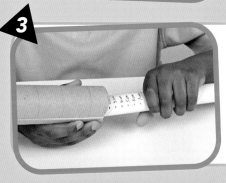

3 Put the wider tube over the narrower tube and pull back to the first mark.

4 Let go of the tube and see what happens. Pull back to the second mark and release then repeat by pulling back to the other marks.

▶ **Observe**
What happened to the elastic band when you pulled the kitchen roll tube back over the other tube?

▶ **Predict**
What will happen as you pull the tube further and further back and then let go?

▶ **What's wrong?**
Rocket doesn't travel far? Try a thicker elastic band.

▶ **Record**
Work out a way to record the distance travelled by the wider tube then repeat the experiment twice more to record your results. What do they show?
Use a camcorder to record the flight of your rocket.

▶ **Think about it**
How could you use a pencil to make a paperclip into an object which springs back into shape when you squash it?

Feel the friction

Try sliding your feet side by side – you have to push quite hard to get going. Once you've started then it's a lot easier. When you try to push at first there is a force between you and the floor. It pushes back and tries to stop you moving. This force is called static friction.

Once you start moving another force called sliding friction pushes against your push. It is weaker than static friction but the moment you stop pushing, static friction takes over and makes you stop moving.

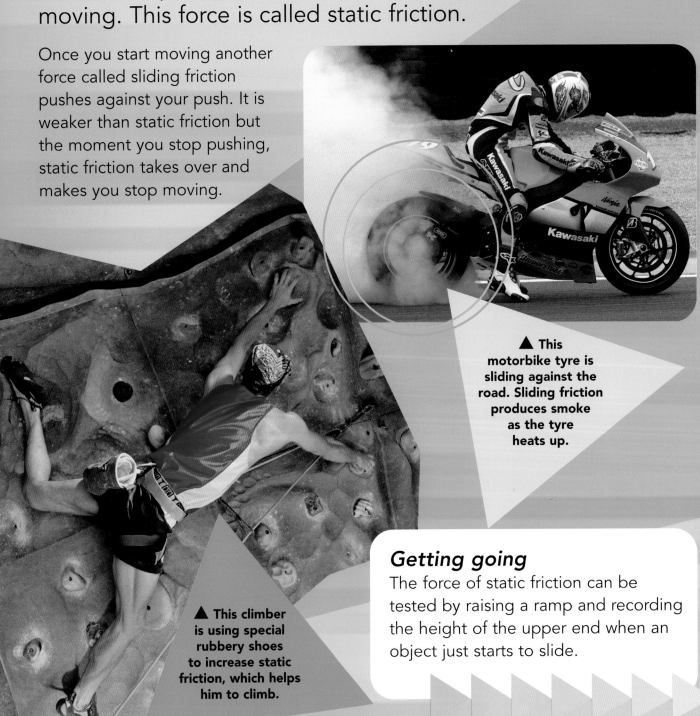

▲ This motorbike tyre is sliding against the road. Sliding friction produces smoke as the tyre heats up.

▲ This climber is using special rubbery shoes to increase static friction, which helps him to climb.

Getting going
The force of static friction can be tested by raising a ramp and recording the height of the upper end when an object just starts to slide.

16

The greatest gripper

Science box

A selection of footwear (for example a trainer, shoe, sandal, boot, slipper), a weight (such as a tin of beans), a short plank of wood or a tray (to make a ramp), books, a ruler, sticky tape, modelling clay.

1

Take your first item of footwear and put the tin of beans in it.

2

Put the footwear on the ramp and raise one end on some books. Tape down the front of the ramp to make a fair test – keep it in position. Fix a ruler at the raised end with some modelling clay.

3

Add books until the footwear just starts to slide. Measure the height of the raised end at this point.

4

Repeat steps 1–3 with your range of footwear.

▶ **Predict**

Which footwear will have the greatest grip and which will have the least?

▶ **Record**

Make a table and record the height of the ramp when each item began to slide. Use a camcorder or mobile phone to show when the greatest gripper and the worst gripper began to slide.

▶ **What's wrong?**

All footwear slide at same height. Try covering the slope with sand paper or a piece of old carpet.

▶ **Extra experiment**

What will happen to the footwear if you soak the ramp in soapy water? Make your predictions and then test them – outside!

▶ **Think about it**

The area of the surfaces in contact does not affect the strength of the friction. If it did, what would happen if you sat up as you started coming down a slide and then laid flat?

Air resistance

The air pushes on anything that moves. This pushing force is called air resistance (drag). If the object is moving slowly the air resistance is low, but as the object moves faster the air resistance becomes stronger. Think about it – you cannot feel air pushing on your face as you walk along, but you can when you cycle down a hill quickly.

The first parachute launch was made from a hydrogen balloon by André Garnerin in 1797. The parachute was attached to the balloon and was released at a height of 800 m. The parachute opened and slowed Garnerin down, but it swung from side to side as the air flowed out from around its edge and made Garnerin sick!

▼ Parachutes are vital for making air drops of supplies to places where planes cannot land.

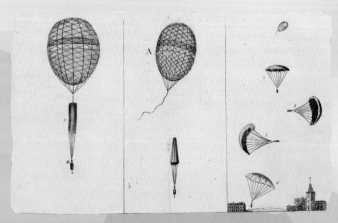

▲ This illustration shows how Garnerin's parachute fell from the balloon and then swung from side to side.

Getting going
You can make a hand-launch parachute by using a flexible plastic bag. This means you don't have to be up high to launch it – unlike Garnerin!

Make a parachute

1 Set the point and pencil in the compasses to a gap of 7 cm. Place the point in the centre of the card and mark out a circle 14 cm in diameter.

Science box

A pair of compasses with pencil, a ruler, a piece of card 16 cm square, a thin 16 cm-square piece of plastic sheet which folds easily, scissors, three cotton threads 15 cm long, sticky tape, two small pieces of modelling clay.

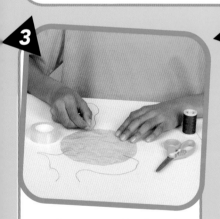

2 Cut out the disc of card and place it on the sheet of plastic. Cut a circle in the plastic sheet using the card to guide you.

3 Stick one end of each thread to the plastic sheet. Make sure they are equally spaced around the circular edge of the sheet.

4 Attach one of the pieces of modelling clay to the other ends of the three threads. Make sure that all the threads have the same length connecting the modelling clay to the edge of the sheet.

▶ **Observe**
Hold up your finished parachute in one hand and a ball of modelling clay in the other. Let them both go. Do they reach the ground together?

▶ **Fair test**
Hold the parachute in the palm of your hand and throw it upwards. Try this a few times. Cut a small hole in the centre of the parachute and repeat the test.

▶ **What's wrong?**
Parachute spinning? Untangle threads before you throw.

▶ **Recording**
Use a camcorder to film the parachute falling without the hole and with the hole.

▶ **Think about it**
Would a hole in Garnerin's parachute have prevented him from being sick?

Water resistance

When a boat moves over the surface of the water its hull rubs against the water as it pushes forwards. The water pushes on the hull in the opposite direction with a force called water resistance (drag). This can slow down the boat and make it harder to move.

▲ High-speed powerboats have long, narrow hulls with gently curved sides. This shape makes water move smoothly over the hull and creates less water resistance.

Getting going

The hull of a boat can be almost any shape. Does the shape of the hull affect the water resistance on it as it moves through the water? If water resistance is low the hull will move quickly, but if the water resistance is high the boat will move slowly.

Boat hull shapes

1

Take the pieces of modelling clay and make them into different shaped hulls – round, square, narrow and very narrow.

Science box

Four pieces of modelling clay, a large bowl or bath filled with some water.

2

Gently place the first hull into the water at one end of the bowl.

3

Flick the hull shape with your finger to move it through the water.

4

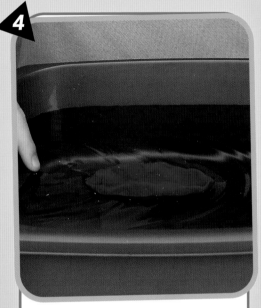

Repeat steps 2–3 with all the hull shapes. Which hull do you think has the least resistance?

▶ **Record**
Film the flicking of the hulls with a camcorder. Watch the video to assess which hull moves through the water the best.

▶ **What's wrong?**
Boat hulls sinking? Change the design, or increase the depth of the hull.

▶ **Fair test**
Use the same amount of modelling clay for each hull. How can you make sure that you flick the hulls with the same amount of force?

▶ **Extra experiment**
Add a small sail to each boat using a cocktail stick for a mast and a piece of paper for a sail. Now repeat steps 2-3 but use a balloon pump to blow on the sail and move the hull. What do you notice about the direction the different hulls travel in?

▶ **Think about it**
Compare your hull shapes with those of real boats and ships, such as speedboats, ferries and tankers. Why aren't all boats the same shape?

Super submarine

When an object is placed in water, two forces act on it. The object's weight pulls it down and the force of the water pushing on it, called the upthrust, pushes up. If the weight is stronger than the upthrust the object sinks. If the weight is less than the upthrust the object floats.

▶ The upthrust on this mini-sub remains the same throughout its trip but its weight can be changed to make it rise and fall as it explores the coral reef.

Getting going

You can see how air and water can make a submarine sink and rise by making your own simple model submarine.

Science box

A 500 ml plastic drinks bottle with flat sides, a piece of plastic tubing about 60 cm long, strong sticky tape, modelling clay, scissors, nine coins, a sink or a deep bowl of water.

1

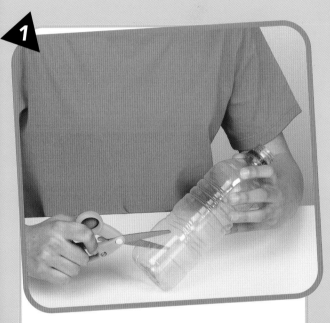

Use the scissors to make two holes in the plastic bottle.

2

Put three piles of three coins on the side where the holes have been made. Hold them in place with sticky tape.

3

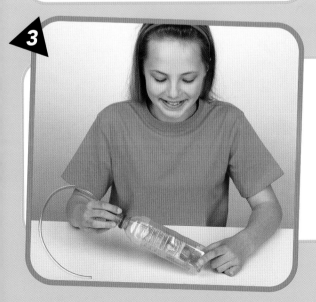

Place one end of the tube inside the bottle so that it reaches the middle of the inside. Continues on the next page...

Super submarine 23

▲ This huge submarine has a crew of 98 and is 97 m long. It weighs 7,800,000 kg, but still sinks and rises using ballast tanks.

Submarine ballast tanks

A submarine can change its weight using air and water so that it can sink and float. Inside a submarine are large containers called ballast tanks. They can contain air or water. When the submarine is floating on the surface of the water, its ballast tanks are full of air but when a dive is ordered, water is pumped in and the air is pushed out. The submarine sinks and an engine powers a propeller at the back to drive it along underwater. When the submarine needs to come to the surface, tanks of compressed air are opened into the ballast tanks. The air pushes the water out and the submarine rises.

4

Push the modelling clay around the tube to keep it inside the bottle.

5

Lower the 'submarine' into the water with coins and holes on top. Wait for the bottle to fill with water, then turn it over so that the coins and holes are underneath.

6

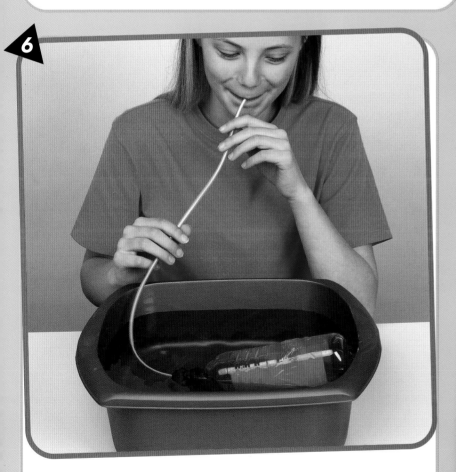

Blow through the tube and watch your submarine rise out of the water!

► **What's wrong?**
Submarine rising too much at one end? Reposition the coins to balance out the weight. Sticky tape coming off in the water? Use stronger tape – or more of it.

► **Observe**
When the submarine is completely underwater:
1) Blow steadily down the tube and watch what happens.

2) Put your finger over the end of the tube to block it and watch what happens now.

3) Remove your finger for a few moments and watch the submarine then cover the hole again.

4) Remove your finger and leave the hole open. What happens to the submarine?

► **Record**
Use a camcorder to record how your submarine sinks and rises.

► **Think about it**
What would happen if the holes were made much bigger? What would happen if you added more coins to the underside of the bottle?

Water power

For thousands of years the push of flowing or falling water has been used to drive machinery. The pushing force in the water is changed into a turning force by a water wheel. Today, water and steam are used to turn blades inside machines called turbines.

◀ These massive blades are inside a steam turbine. Super-heated water gives off steam, which pushes on the blades.

Some of the electricity we use is generated by turbines. As the turbine turns, its axle spins a magnet round in a case full of wires. The spinning magnet generates electricity in the wires, which is carried through cables to power lights and homes in towns and cities.

Getting going
In the past, water wheels could also be used to raise things, such as sacks of flour. See if you can make a water wheel that can raise an object.

Make a water wheel

1

Shape the large piece of modelling clay around the middle of the pencil.

2

Use sticky tape to fasten one end of the thread to the pencil. Put the small piece of modelling clay (the object) on the other end.

3

Cut out plastic blades about 5 cm by 10 cm from the butter tub lids.

4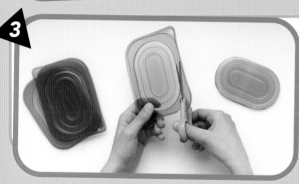

Stick the blades into the modelling clay on the pencil. Slide on the pieces of cardboard tube. Hold the tube pieces and blades over the bowl. Get a friend to slowly pour the water onto the blades.

Science box

Two pieces of modelling clay (one large, one small), a pencil, four plastic lids (such as those used on butter tubs), scissors, a piece of thread 16 cm long, a small cardboard tube cut into short lengths (an empty clingfilm one will do), sticky tape, a bottle of water and a bowl – and a friend!

▶ **What's wrong?**
Blades fall out? Water flowing too fast – add more clay to pencil. No movement of wheel? Water not flowing fast enough!

▶ **Observe**
What happens to the wheel when you put it in the stream of water? What happens to the small ball of clay?

▶ **Predict**
Add four more blades and predict what will happen when you put the wheel back in the stream of water. Test your prediction.

▶ **Recording**
Use a camcorder to film your water wheel in action.

▶ **Think about it**
What is the force that is really moving the water wheel?

Page 7 Zig zag ramps

The table tennis ball will go fast down a steep slope and slower down a less steep slope. The rolling ball will knock the hanging table tennis ball and it will swing out. Gravity pulls the hanging ball backwards and forwards until it stops swinging. The hanging ball may hardly swing at all when the slow moving ball hits it. It could stop the rolling ball moving if the table tennis ball is moving very slowly. The ramps let the skate boarders build up speed by using gravity to pull them down.

Page 9 Testing for balance

The bottle can be tilted to a greater angle before it falls over when the amount of water in the bottle is small. As more water is added its centre of gravity rises and it falls over at a smaller angle of tilt. If the bottle was turned upside down it would rest on its cap which makes a smaller base than the bottom of the bottle. This would make the bottle tilt over at a smaller angle before it fell because its weight soon pushes down outside its base.

Page 11 Bridge strength

The thin card bridge should collapse with a smaller weight pressing on it than the corrugated cardboard bridge. If a cardboard bridge is made with the corrugations running the length of the bridge instead of across it, the bridge will be found to be stronger than the other two. When the corrugations run parallel to the bridge supports (the cereal packets) they behave as little arches and give extra strength. When they run lengthways they behave as tubes and give even more strength.

Page 13 Magnet power

When you move the magnet, the paperclip and screw will move too. They will keep close to the end of the magnet on the other side of the card. If you move the magnet quickly you may move the paperclip and screw out of the magnetic field and they will fall away. It is likely the screw will fall first because it is heavier. The magnetic force is pulling against gravity.

Page 15 Elastic band rocket

The elastic band stretches as you pull back one tube over the other. The further you pull back the tube the further it goes when you release it due to the tension force which is created in the elastic band. You could record how far the rocket travelled before it fell to the ground – make sure you stand in the same position when you launch it. The paperclip could be bent around the pencil to make a coil which behaves like a spring.

Page 17 The greatest gripper

The footwear with the roughest surface will have the greatest grip and the footwear with the smoothest surface will have the weakest grip. If the surface is wet the water fills up the hollows and makes the surface smoother so the force of friction is weaker. If friction was affected by the area of surfaces in contact, when you laid back you would have a larger area in contact with the slide and you would slow down and perhaps stop – but friction isn't affected, so there is no change of speed.

Page 19 Make a parachute

The ball of modelling clay falls faster than the parachute. The parachute without the hole swings about. The parachute with the hole falls more steadily. After his first test, Garnerin actually had a hole put in his parachute so it did not swing about and make him sick.

Page 21 Boat hull shapes

The hulls need to be made with high sides to stop them sinking when they are flicked. The very narrow hull has the least water resistance followed by the narrow, round and square hull. The same fingers should be flicked to keep the test fair. If a sail and balloon pump is used the hulls with the pointed fronts will sail a more precise path than the round and square fronts. The hulls of ships and boats are different because they are designed to do different jobs. A ferry, for example, may have a square front so that it can have doors present to allow vehicles on and off the ship.

Page 25 Make a model submarine

When you blow steadily, you push water out of the submarine and it begins to rise. When you block the air tube with your finger, the air in the submarine cannot escape so the submarine floats. When you remove your finger air comes out of the tube and water rushes back into the submarine to replace it. This makes the submarine begin to sink but it stops when you replace your finger and block the hole. When you remove your finger again the submarine continues to sink until it reaches the bottom of the bowl. The submarine would lose air faster and sink faster if the holes were bigger. If you add more coins they may make the submarine too heavy and it will not rise when you blow air in.

Page 27 Make a water wheel

The water wheel may turn a couple of times or perhaps make only half a turn. The weight on the string will rise as the string coils round the pencil. When four more blades are added the water wheel will turn more quickly and keep turning for longer, the weight may be raised up to the pencil more quickly and the blades will make more splashes! The falling water is being pulled down by gravity.

Further information

Look at these websites for more information on forces and how they move things:

▶ *http://www.science-experiments.info/ Kids_Gravity_Experiments.html*
This website shows a video of a simple gravity experiment which you can try and see if you get the same results.

▶ *http://pbskids.org/zoom/activities/sci/ parachute.html*
Design, make and test your own plastic bag parachute.

▶ *http://www.kids-science-experiments.com/invisibleforce.html*
Try to move a toy car using two magnets in this experiment.

▶ *http://www.bbc.co.uk/learningzone/ clips/testing-air-resistance/1634.html*
Link to part of the BBC website showing video clips. In this example, at the Leaning Tower of Pisa, the question "Do heavier objects fall faster than lighter objects?" is tested.

▶ *http://www.hometrainingtools.com/articles/ water-wheel-science-project.html*
You may like to make a larger water wheel on a stand. Look at this website and scroll down to the picture of the finished water wheel. Read through the instructions with an adult and ask him or her to help you make it.

▶ *http://www.bbc.co.uk/schools/ks2bitesize/ science/physical_processes/forces/play.shtml*
Play games on the BBC Bitesize website to test your understanding of forces.

▶ *http://www.highhopes.com/ maverickboats.html*
Make paper boats using this website and compare how they move through the water against the boats you made on page 21.

▶ *http://www.fatlion.com/science/cartesian.html*
Make a diver go up and down by trying the experiment on this website.

▶ *http://www.sciencekids.co.nz/ gamesactivities/forcesinaction.html*
Can you use weights to make the truck travel to the end of the track?
Try the simple experiment at this website.

Every effort has been made by the Publishers to ensure that these websites contain no inappropriate or offensive material. However, because of the nature of the Internet, it is impossible to guarantee that the contents of these sites will not be altered. We strongly advise that Internet access is supervised by a responsible adult.

Glossary

Axle
A long, round bar that turns on a machine to which wheels or other devices, such as turbine blades, are attached.

Ballast
A material on a ship (stones or concrete) or submarine (air and water) that makes the vessel easier to control.

Cables
Long, thick, strong wires used for holding things in place.

Centre of gravity
The place inside an object where all the weight seems to pull down from.

Compressed (air)
Squashed to make fit in a smaller space.

Drag
A force that acts in the opposite direction to the one in which an object is moving in air or water.

Elastic
The property of a material that allows it to be stretched, but return to its original length when released.

Friction (sliding)
The frictional force that acts between two surfaces as they slide over each other.

Friction (static)
The frictional force that stops one surface moving over another when the first surface is given a gentle push.

Gravity
The force that tries to pull things towards each other and holds us on the Earth's surface – without it we would fly off into space!

Hull
The part of a ship or boat that is in contact with the water.

Hydrogen
A gas found in very small amounts in the Earth's atmosphere.

Magnetic
Able to attract iron and steel to its surface.

Nuclear
This word relates to the nucleus; a central part of an atom. Atoms are very tiny particles that make up all materials.

Predict
Say what will happen next after thinking about the experiment you are about to make.

Resistance
A force that acts in the opposite direction to another force.

Speed
A measure of the distance travelled in a certain time as an object moves along.

Tension
A force that is generated in an object when it is stretched and acts in the opposite direction to the stretching force.

Turbine
A machine that turns using the force of water, air or steam.

Upthrust
A pushing force made by water on an object that has entered it.

Weight
The force of an object pressing down towards the centre of the Earth because of the effect of gravity.

Index

To my granddaughter
Pippa May

This edition 2012

First published in 2008 by
Franklin Watts
338 Euston Road
London NW1 3BH

Franklin Watts Australia
Level 17/207 Kent Street
Sydney NSW 2000

Text © Peter Riley 2008
Design and Concept © Franklin Watts 2008

All rights reserved.

Series editor: Adrian Cole
Art Director: Jonathan Hair
Design: Matthew Lilly
Picture Research: Diana Morris
Photography: Andy Crawford (unless
otherwise credited)

Acknowledgements:
BAE Systems/Getty Images: 24. Manfred
Bail/Alamy: 3cr, 22. C L Claire/A1 Pix: 8bl.
David Finch www.judophotos.com: 2c, 8c.
Getty Images : 1, 3cl, 20. Peter Ginter/Getty
Images: 13t. Laurence Gough/Shutterstock:
2tl, 5t. Valery Hache/Getty Images: 16tr.
Brownie Harris/Corbis: 26. MJ Kim/Getty
Images: 6. Natali a Kolesnikova/AFP/Getty
Images: 14bl. Jimin Lai/AFP/Getty Images:
4t. Dennis Macdonald/Alamy: 4b. Jamie
McDonald/Getty Images: 2br, 14tr. NASA:
12-13 background. Frank Rossotto/Getty
Images: 18t. Science Museum/Science &
Society PL: 18bl. Shutterstock/Harper: cover
cr. Shutterstock/Juri Samsonov: cover ct.
Shutterstock/Morgan Lane Photography:
cover cl.Shutterstock/Rafael Ramirez Lee:
cover tr. Shutterstock/Sonja Foos: cover br.
Shutterstock/Thomas Mounsey: cover bl.
Shutterstock/yuork: cover tl. Stas
Volik/istockphoto: 10. Michael Wong/Getty
Images: 16bl.

Every attempt has been made to clear
copyright. Should there be any inadvertent
omission please apply
to the publisher for rectification.

A CIP catalogue record for this
book is available from the
British Library.

Dewey number: 530.4

ISBN: 978 1 4451 0731 8

Printed in China

Franklin Watts is a division of
Hachette Children's Books,
an Hachette UK company.
www.hachette.co.uk